You Know You're Getting Old When...

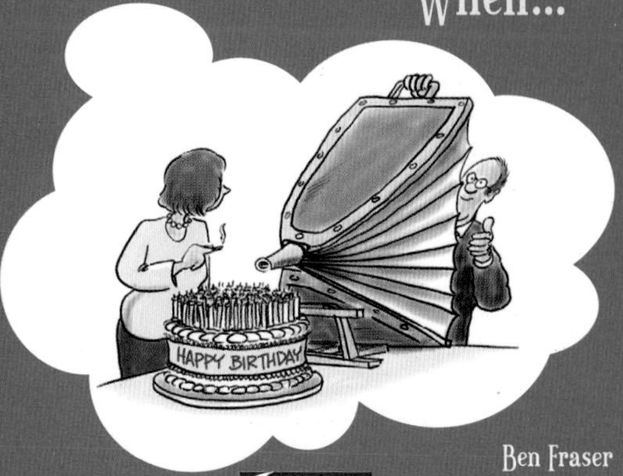

Ben Fraser

summersdale

YOU KNOW YOU'RE GETTING OLD WHEN...

First published in 2003
This edition copyright © Summersdale Publishers Ltd 2009

Illustrations by Roger Penwill

Summersdale Publishers Ltd
46 West Street
Chichester
West Sussex
PO19 1RP
UK

www.summersdale.com

Printed and bound in China

ISBN: 978-1-84953-005-7

Substantial discounts on bulk quantities of Summersdale books are available to corporations, professional associations and other organisations. For details telephone Summersdale Publishers on (+44-1243-771107), fax (+44-1243-786300) or email (nicky@summersdale.com).

You Know You're
Getting Old
When...

You know there was something you wanted to complain about, you just can't remember what it was.

Your birthday party gets a little wild
and you apologise to the neighbours,
only to find out they hadn't
even noticed.

Life without sex would be tolerable, but life without glasses impossible.

You doze off on the bus, and people think you've passed away.

Most of your body hurts. If any bits don't hurt, it's because they've stopped working.

Your house is too big to live in but your medicine cupboard is far too small to hold all your pills.

You know everything worth knowing.
If only someone would actually
ask you about it.

'Getting some action' mainly involves
buying a pack of laxatives.

You find a song that shook the world in the wild days of your youth in the Easy Listening section of the shop.

There is more hair up your
nose than on your head.

You want people to remember your
birthday but forget how many
of them you've had.

You used to go to bed at dawn,
but now that's when you get up.

19

You have to choose between tearing off all your clothes and making passionate love – you haven't the energy for both.

You think you have a totally clear
conscience, but in fact you just
have a very poor memory.

Getting up from the armchair
generally requires more
than two attempts.

People start telling you that you
look young... for your age.

You can keep house plants alive for more than a month – in fact you have house plants that are applying for their pension.

You lose track of your last stubborn
dark hair – it's gone over to
the grey side.

By the time you've had a bit of a rest,
you've forgotten what it was that tired
you out in the first place.

Middle-aged people give up their seats for you on the bus.

Those toys you had as a child that you buried in the garden are now worth a fortune.

You hear yourself passing on advice
to your children that your
parents gave you.

You think about the cost of going out for a few drinks and decide to stay in and watch TV instead.

You can be trusted with a
secret because you won't
remember it anyway.

You stop looking for products with a Lifetime Guarantee and settle instead for a Two-Year Guarantee.

You feel a sense of triumph when you remember what you went upstairs for.

Your life insurance premium is higher
than your mortgage payments.

You find yourself being chauffeured everywhere – because people think your driving is a public hazard.

You get pulled aside at airports due to the amount of metal in your replacement joints.

You wish you'd given in to temptation a
bit more while you had the chance.

Helping little old ladies across the street is no longer a good deed, but what happens whenever you go out with friends.

You find yourself repeating things
over and over.

You find yourself repeating...
oh, hang on.

You get stopped by the police for driving too slowly instead of too fast.

You've mastered the secrets of the
universe – but you can't
remember them.

You and your friends understand the comparative benefits of various pension schemes – in fact that's your favourite topic of conversation.

It can take you days to remember where you left the car – or what it looks like.

You feel comfortable telling everyone
you meet exactly what you
think of them.

You pull your hair into a tight bun...
to keep your face in place.

The phone rings and you answer the remote control... or any other nearby object.

Your heart beats faster when you see a certain someone – it's your GP...

Your childhood decades go from being classified as 'retro' to 'ancient history'.

You use a mail·order dentist – you send them your teeth and they come back as good as new...

You accept or reject social invitations
based on whether they finish
'at a sensible time'.

You come across a speed hump while
driving and have to reverse
and take a run up.

You can get away with almost
anything – the public mischief
charges would never stand up in court.

You are let free first from a group of
hostages because your captors
feel sorry for you.

You need a hurricane to blow out all the candles on your birthday cake.

The car you have now cost you as
much as your first house did.

You could legally marry someone half your age. And they could legally marry someone half their age.

You need a cine-film projector to watch your home movies.

Not wearing a bra causes
chafing on your knees.

You start every sentence with,
'During the war...'

It is no longer possible to get that replacement part for your gramophone.

You feel the need to iron
your handkerchiefs.

You dread surprise parties.
Your heart just can't take it.

Your family ask casually what
kind of funeral music you like.

You no longer see the need for shoes...
you have slippers.

Most of your clothes are hand-made
— you've knitted them yourself.

You find a new passion in your life:
the game of bowls.

Your family apologise for keeping you up if they phone after dinner.

You find everything on the TV rude,
crude or lewd – including
the kids' programmes.

You refer to nightclubs
as discotheques.

Someone calls to sell you a timeshare apartment and you tell them all about the last time you went abroad with Auntie Mabel.

Rowntree's Fruit Gums are simply
out of the question.

You feel no shame in talking about your bowels at great length.

You have a selection of walking stick
designs to match your outfits.

You don't need to go to a bar to meet
your friends – they're all on
the bus into town!

You have acquired a new language
of mutters and tuts.

The gap between your belt and your
armpits is considerably smaller
than it used to be.

You spend five hours doing
your weekly food shopping.

Your idea of a wild night in with your partner is listening to classical music with the lights off.

Have you enjoyed this book?
If so, why not write a review
on your favourite website?

Thanks very much for buying
this Summersdale book.

www.summersdale.com